Scary Creatures
ALLIGATORS
and CROCODILES

Written by
Dr. Gerald Legg

Illustrated by
Nicholas Hewetson

Created and designed by
David Salariya

W
FRANKLIN WATTS
A Division of Scholastic Inc.
NEW YORK • TORONTO • LONDON • AUCKLAND • SYDNEY
MEXICO CITY • NEW DELHI • HONG KONG
DANBURY, CONNECTICUT

Author:

Dr. Gerald Legg holds a doctorate in
zoology from Manchester University. He worked in
West Africa for several years as a lecturer and
rainforest researcher. His current position is biologist
at the Booth Museum of Natural History in Brighton,
England.

Artist:

Nicholas Hewetson was educated in
Sussex at Brighton Technical School and studied
illustration at Eastbourne College of Art. He has since
illustrated a wide variety of children's books.

Additional Artists:
Mark Bergin
Emily Mayer
Carolyn Scrace
David Stewart
Shirley Willis

Series Creator:

David Salariya was born in Dundee,
Scotland. In 1989 he established The Salariya Book
Company. He has illustrated a wide range of books
and has created many new series for publishers in the
U.K. and overseas. He lives in Brighton with his wife,
illustrator Shirley Willis, and their son.

Editor: Karen Barker Smith

Picture Research: Nicky Roe

Created, designed, and produced by
The Salariya Book Company Ltd
Book House
25 Marlborough Place
Brighton BN1 1UB

Visit the Salariya Book Company at
www.salariya.com

A CIP catalog record for this title is available
from the Library of Congress.

ISBN 0-531-14670-7 (Lib. Bdg.)
ISBN 0-531-14848-3 (Pbk.)

Published in the United States by Franklin Watts
A Division of Scholastic Inc.
90 Sherman Turnpike
Danbury, CT 06816

Reprinted in China in 2006.

Printed on paper from sustainable forests.

Photo Credits:

t=top, b=bottom

ANT Photo Gallery, NHPA: 13
Anthony Bannister, NHPA: 17
Corbis Images: 8, 9
Martin Harvey, NHPA: 12
PhotoDisc: 10, 21, 25
Salariya Book Company: 23t
J & A Scott, NHPA: 14
Martin Wendler, NHPA: 22, 23b

Contents

What Are Alligators and Crocodiles?

Alligators, crocodiles, caiman, and gavials are all crocodilians. They are reptiles that live in water and are related to lizards, snakes, tortoises, and turtles. Crocodilians were alive when dinosaurs walked the Earth. Today there are about 23 different **species**.

Are lizards crocodilians?

Gecko

Lizards are reptiles but are not crocodilians. They have a different type of skull and heart as well as other parts.

No, lizards are not crocodilians.

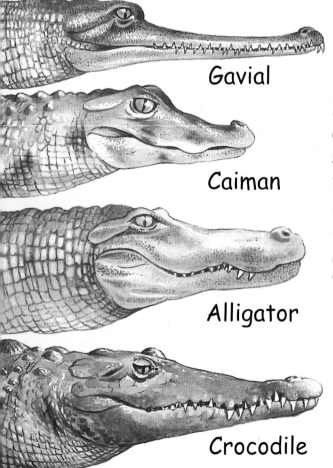

Gavial

Caiman

Alligator

Crocodile

It can be difficult to tell the difference between types of crocodilians. When a crocodile's mouth is closed some of its teeth slide into a C-shaped groove on either side of the top jaw. The teeth can be seen when the mouth is closed. Alligators and caiman don't have these grooves so the teeth in the same position cannot be seen when their mouths are fully closed.

X-Ray Vision

Hold the next page up to the light and see what's inside a crocodile.

See what's inside

strong tail

ribs

short, powerful legs

large skull

sharp teeth

What's Inside a Crocodilian?

The skeleton of a crocodilian is long and flexible, making it **streamlined**. The eyes and nostrils are located high up on the long, pointed skull, letting the animal see and breathe when the rest of its body is **submerged**. A powerful, muscular tail propels crocodilians through the water when it is swimming.

Did You Know?

Crocodiles can replace their teeth. When an old tooth is lost, a new one grows from below to replace it. A 13-foot long Nile crocodile can go through more than 45 sets of teeth in its lifetime.

old tooth

new tooth

Cutaway of a crocodile to show its organs

The lower chamber of the heart is almost completely divided into two halves. This makes a crocodilian's blood circulation more efficient than other reptiles.

lungs

intestines

heart

liver

stomach

webbed toes

nostrils

crocodile's upper jaw

A good sense of smell helps crocodilians find **prey** hiding in murky water. They also have sense organs on scales located along the sides of their jaws that help with this.

How Do Crocodilians See, Hear, and Smell?

Most crocodilians' are **nocturnal** and their eyes are designed to help them hunt at night. A slit-like, vertical **pupil** lets more light in and a mirror-like layer at the back of the eye shines light back on to the **retina**. Since crocodilians have **binocular vision** they can also judge distances, which is very important for a **predator**.

Crocodile on a river bank, watching for prey

Alligator swimming partly submerged

A special see-through eyelid
protects a crocodilian's eyes
when the animal is underwater.

Did You Know?

Crocodiles have good
hearing. Flaps cover the
ear openings to protect
the ears when a
crocodile is underwater.

A crocodile floating almost submerged (left) can leap out of the water in a flash to catch a bird flying several feet above it.

How Do Crocodilians Move?

On land, crocodilians crawl on their stomach or lift it off the ground and do the "high walk," dragging their tail behind them. If alarmed, they walk then slide down a slope into the water. Crocodilians can also gallop. They lift their body off of the ground and they sweep their tails from side to side.

Crocodilians tuck their front legs into the sides of their body when swimming. They use their tails to propel themselves through the water (right).

Crocodilians are **amphibious**. They are excellent swimmers and use their powerful tails to speed them through the water. The tail sweeps from side to side in a rippling, s-shaped pattern. Many crocodilians have webbed feet but their legs are usually held close to the body and are not used when swimming.

With its stomach touching the ground, a crocodilian slowly crawls along. They can speed up to a gallop, reaching about 11 mph (18 kph) (below).

Where Do Crocodilians Live?

Crocodilians can only live in **tropical** and **subtropical** areas. Since they are cold-blooded, they need to bask in the sun to warm up. They live close to water where they have a ready supply of food. They can live in large rivers or small streams, marshes, swamps, ponds, creeks, and by the sea. Crocodiles cool off by submerging in water.

Did You Know?

The small reservoir at Sierra Leone University in Africa was home to several West African dwarf crocodiles – until some of the gardeners caught and ate them!

Saltwater, or estuarine, crocodile basking

Did You Know?

At cool and dry times of the year crocodilians often hide away in burrows or in quiet ponds and don't eat. They wait there until the weather gets better.

Saltwater crocodile on a river bed

What Do Crocodilians Eat?

Crocodilians are **carnivores**. Small or young crocodilians eat insects, crayfish, crabs, frogs, and small fish. As they grow bigger they can catch larger prey, including small mammals, lizards, snakes, turtles, and birds. Large crocodilians will even catch wildebeest, zebras, monkeys, deer, and people. Crocodilians don't always catch live prey – they will happily eat **carrion**.

14 Nile crocodiles eating a zebra

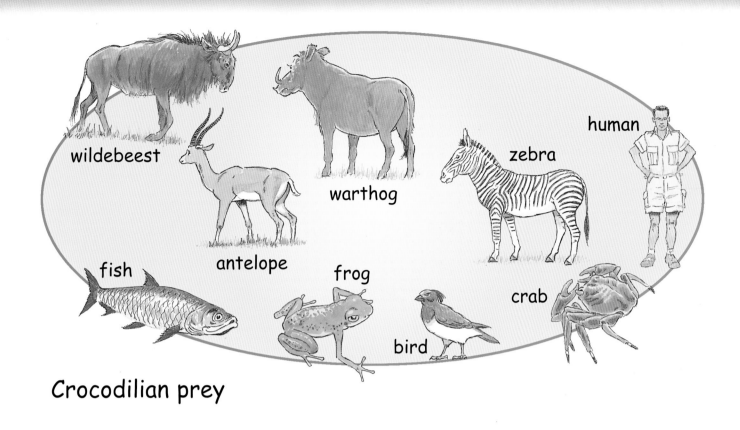

Crocodilian prey

Crocodilians don't need to eat very often. One alligator was known to survive 1,591 days without eating. A large crocodilian will usually feast once a week. It takes several days for the meal to **digest**.

Odd things have been found inside alligators' and crocodiles' stomachs, including license plates, spears, kettles, bullets, and food cans.

 Did You Know?

The Cuban crocodile can snatch perching birds from the branches of trees that overhang rivers.

How Do Crocodilians Hunt?

Crocodilians are fierce hunters. **Hatchlings** snap at insects, small fish, and frogs. Older animals wait for and **stalk** their prey. Large prey is grabbed by the crocodilian's powerful jaws and dragged underwater where it drowns. The crocodilian grips its prey hard and spins it fast to make sure the prey is dead. This also helps rip the prey to pieces.

Many crocodilians eat stones (above). The stones help to grind up food in the stomach and are called gastroliths.

Many crocodilians store their dead prey underwater where it rots and becomes tender to eat.

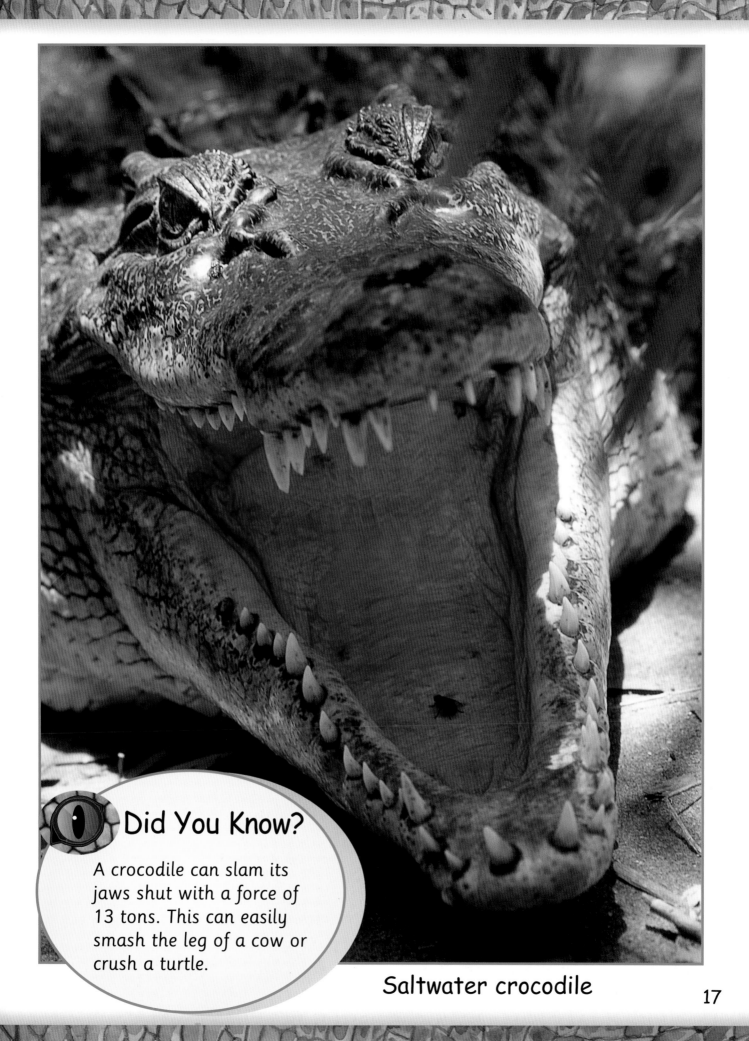

Did You Know?

A crocodile can slam its jaws shut with a force of 13 tons. This can easily smash the leg of a cow or crush a turtle.

Saltwater crocodile

Do Crocodilians Lay Eggs?

Male and female crocodilians mate underwater. A few weeks later, the female makes a nest at night. This can be a hole dug in the ground or a mound of earth or vegetation. The eggs are kept warm by the sun, or by the heat given off from rotting plants.

Female crocodilians guard their nests. When the eggs hatch, they carefully carry the young to the water for safety.

Depending on the age and species of crocodilian, between 10 and 60 eggs are laid (left). They hatch between 50 and 115 days later.

X-Ray Vision

Hold the next page up to the light and see what's inside crocodile eggs.

See what's inside

Do Crocodilians Have Enemies?

Except for people, few animals will attack an adult crocodilian. Jaguars are known to attack nesting females. If a crocodile gets in the way of an elephant, lion, hippopotamus, or rhinoceros it might be attacked. Some large snakes, such as the anaconda, will feed on crocodilians. Crocodilian eggs are eaten by monitor lizards and the hatchlings are at risk from birds such as the marabou stork.

Crocodilians will fight each other sometimes (right).

 Did You Know?

If baby crocodiles are in danger, their mother may pick them up and keep them in her mouth pouch for safety.

Why Do People Kill Crocodilians?

It is hard for crocodilians to live near humans. People are frightened of them and will kill them because several species of crocodilian attack people. Around 2,000 people each year are killed by alligators and crocodiles. However, most crocodilians keep away from humans and are harmless.

Did You Know?

Crocodilians are also hunted for their skins. Each year thousands of illegal, stuffed crocodilians, skins, and other products are **confiscated** by government officials throughout the world.

Confiscated caiman skins in South America

Crocodilian skin is made into bags, shoes, wallets, clothes, and belts. There is no need to kill crocodilians when other materials can be made to look just like real skin.

In tropical and subtropical areas, tourists may find all kinds of things for sale made from illegally killed crocodilians, such as this hideous pen holder (below).

Confiscated pen holder with an illegal stuffed crocodile head

Crocodilian Stories and Legends

Crocodilians have become part of the folklore of many cultures because of their large size and fierce nature. They have been worshiped as gods and linked with the origins of people. They have also been the source of some dragon legends. In the past, crocodilians were often feared as evil monsters and killed.

Sebek

In ancient Egypt, crocodiles were honored and kept in ponds. The larger ones had their foreheads decorated. The Egyptians worshiped a crocodile-headed god called Sebek (right), who was believed to carry dead kings to the underworld.

Aboriginal picture of a crocodile

In several cultures crocodiles are believed to have given birth to humankind. They are part of creation myths. This picture (left), based on Australian Aboriginal rock art, shows such a crocodile.

The stories of European dragons in the Middle Ages told of fire-breathing, people-eating monsters. These fierce dragons were feared because they brought disaster and death. Some pictures of them (right) are believed to be based on Nile crocodiles.

European image of a dragon

Chinese dragons seem to be made up of parts of crocodilians and cobra snakes. These wise and powerful dragons are important in Chinese mythology. They were often shown on pottery, clothes, and ornaments such as this vase (below).

In parts of Africa, keeping crocodile teeth is believed to protect against crocodile attacks, lightning, evil spirits, and illness, as well as bring good luck.

How Old Are Crocodilians?

Crocodiles are the closest living relatives of the **extinct** dinosaurs which roamed the Earth over 200 million years ago.

One hundred and ten million years ago there were dinosaur-eating crocodiles. Remains of the super-crocodile Sarcosuchus (right) were discovered in 1997 in the Sahara Desert. The teeth of another, called Deinosuchus, were found in 1858. Deinosuchus roamed North America from New Jersey to Montana.

Protosuchus (left) lived over 200 million years ago in North America. This 3-foot (1-m)-long hunter had dagger-like teeth and was a fast runner and swimmer. Protosuchus was another ancestor of today's crocodilians.

Protosuchus

Stenosaurus fossils

Did You Know?

The oldest known crocodile died in 1997 in a Russian zoo, at age 115. Nile crocodiles can live to 45 in the wild and up to 80 years in **captivity**.

Stenosaurus is an ancestor of the gavial. Stenosaurus lived 200-145 million years ago.

Sarcosuchus

Sarcosuchus (above) was a giant animal which was about the length of a bus. At 50-60 years old it reached its full size of 36-39 feet (11-12 m) and weighed 8 tons.

27

Crocodilians Around the World

Crocodilians live in the tropics and subtropics of the world – the areas around the Equator where it is always hot.

American alligator

American alligators like swamps and marshes, but also live in rivers, lakes, and ponds in the southeastern United States.

Cuvier's dwarf caiman

Cuvier's dwarf caiman is the smallest crocodilian. It lives in the forest rivers of tropical South America.

The common caiman is found in Central and South America, Mexico, the U.S., the West Indies, Cuba, and Puerto Rico.

Common caiman

Indo-Pacific crocodile

The Indo-Pacific crocodile is also called the Australian saltwater crocodile. It travels long distances by sea and can be found from Australia to India, Vietnam, China, New Guinea, and the Solomon Islands.

Gavials are also called gharials. These long-nosed, **endangered** crocodilians live in the rivers of Northern India. They are mainly aquatic and find walking on land difficult.

Gavial

Crocodilian Facts

When fish are **migrating**, crocodiles work together to catch them. They form a semi-circle across the river and herd the fish into a group. Then they eat the fish closest to them.

Nile crocodiles live throughout much of Africa. They are not fussy about where they live and can be found in lakes, rivers, and swamps.

Cuban crocodiles are only found in the Lanier and Zapata swamps of Cuba and are now endangered.

The rounded end of the gavial's snout is probably used to make sounds during mating.

The saltwater crocodile is the largest living species, reaching over 30 feet (9 m) in length.

An adult male alligator will bellow out a warning if it hears a car horn or similar noise. The sound makes the animal think there is a rival in its territory.

The word alligator comes from the Spanish word "el lagarto," which means "the lizard." Caiman is a Spanish word for any type of crocodilian.

Nile crocodiles are the most common predator in Africa. One hundred years ago, about 3,000 people were killed by these crocodiles each year.

More than 40 people were eaten by saltwater crocodiles when a boat sank in a river in Celebes, Indonesia.

To pretend to be sad can be called "crocodile tears." In fact, crocodiles cannot cry but the shiny skin around their eyes can look like tears.

One Nile crocodile was found to have tried to eat too big of a meal – it died with a turtle stuck in its throat.

In 1944, saltwater crocodiles were thought to have killed hundreds of Japanese soldiers overnight.

Glossary

amphibious To live both in water and on land.

binocular vision The ability to see the same area with both eyes at the same time.

captivity To be kept in a man-made environment, such as a zoo.

carnivore Any animal that eats the flesh of other animals as its main food source.

carrion Dead animals and decaying flesh.

confiscate To take banned items away from someone.

digest To pass food through the body.

endangered Animals that are few in numbers and may be close to extinction.

extinct Species of animals that are no longer alive anywhere in the world.

hatchlings Young just hatched from their eggs.

migrating The movement of animals from one place to another to find food or better conditions.

nocturnal An animal that is active at night.

predator Any animal that hunts other living creatures for food.

prey Any animal that is hunted by other animals for food.

pupil The opening in the eye where light passes through to the retina.

retina The part of the eye at the back that is sensitive to light. The retina sends the sensation of vision to the brain.

species A group of living things that look alike, behave in the same way, and can interbreed.

stalking To creep up on prey quietly.

streamlined Made to move through air or water more easily.

submerge To sink or dive below the water's surface.

subtropical Areas of the world that are just outside the tropics but still have a hot climate.

tropical The area of the world near the Equator, where it is always hot.

Index